Shore Lines

Poems from the Water's Edge

by

Philip E. Burnham, Jr.

Ibbetson Street Press

©2012 Philip E. Burnham, Jr.

www.pebjr.com

Book and cover design by S. Glines

Ibbetson Street Press
25 School Street
Somerville MA 02143

www.ibbetsonpress.com

ISBN 978-0-9846614-9-7

All rights reserved including the right to reproduce this work in any form except as provided by U.S. Copyright law.

For information contact the publisher.
Ibbetson Street Press
Printing October 2012
Printed in the United States of America

In memory of my parents

Nella Louise Barber Burnham and Philip Edward Burnham

And for their great-grandson Malakai McGrath Burnham

Acknowledgments

The following poems have been published or accepted for publication in print or on-line journals.

The Aurorean - Fog at Round Pond Maine
Bagelbards' Anthologies # 3, 4 & 6 - Victory Garden, Thanksgiving, Legacy
Blue Unicorn - Perpetual Calendar
The Deronda Review - Candlemas (February 2), The Chapel of St. Gabriel near Tarascon
Emerald Necklace Newsletter - Birthday Greetings VI: The Riverway
Home: An Anthology - Before You Left
Ibbetson Street - Birches in a Country Churchyard, Shelves of War: The Reading Room of the Cork City Library
Journey: An Anthology - From Berkeley to Boston
Lyric - On Pemaquid Beach: The Lost Soldier, 1960 Wedding Photograph
New Arcadia Review – Walking in Paris, Paris en balade
Seventh Quarry - Watercolor Words, Iamque Vale, Hearts of Stone, Cloth of Gold: Round Pond, Maine
Wilderness House - After Isaiah 10:19

I want to thank Christine Cleary and Nancy Haslett for their editorial assistance in assembling and reading this manuscript, Doug Holder for his support of poetry in the Boston area as the founder of the Ibbetson Street Press and Steve Glines for his technical expertise in publishing.

The cover painting is by Philippe Dequesne, and is used with his permission.
The end drawing is by Louise Hassel Burnham.

The photograph of the author is by Christine Cleary.

Table of Contents

Shore Lines

Fog at Round Pond, Maine	3
Watercolor Words	4
Waiting for the Red-winged Blackbirds	5
A Little Boat, My Heart	6
Nohaval Cove, County Cork	7
On Pemaquid Beach: The Lost Soldier	8
Cloth of Gold: Round Pond, Maine	9
From Berkeley to Boston	10
Good morning, Alice!	11
Goat Island, County Waterford	12
A Dream of Fishes	13
Beach Stones	14
Benevolence	15
September Evening at Randlett Pond	16
A Walk at World's End	17
First and Last Paintings, Juxtaposed	*18*
Reluctance	20

Iamque Vale
(And now, Farewell)

Iamque vale	23
Shelves of War:	
The Reading Room of the Cork City Library	24
Fire and Ash	25
Window Boxes, 34 rue des Plantes 1996/2009	26
The Last Time You Saw Paris (2001)	27
Familiar Gestures	28
Before You Left	29
Birches in a Country Churchyard	30
After Isaiah 10:19	*31*
The Roman Amphitheatre at Arles	32
Night Watch, Amsterdam	33
1960 Wedding Photograph	34
Anniversary - 1961	35

Love's Fire

Love's Fire	39
Birthday Greetings VI: The Riverway	40
"Love One Another"	41
Hearts of Stone	42
A Geology of Love	43
Shall We Not Kiss?	44
Is There A Rose?	45
Birthday Greetings V: At the Berlin Zoo	46
Col des Vents 2001	48
The Chapel of Saint Gabriel near Tarascon	49
The Courtyard at the Faculty of Medicine, Montpellier, France	50
The Pont du Gard	51
I Did Not Meet Her in the Morning	52

Thanksgiving

Thanksgiving	55
St Patrick's Hill	56
Waiting for Snow	57
Snowbound	58
Legacy	59
Perpetual Calendar	60
Candlemas (February 2nd)	61
Departure's Space	62
Walking in Paris	63
Paris en balade	64
Ordinary Things: Pompeii	65
Lessons in Greek	66
My Father's Grammar	67
Victory Garden	68
Ibn Khallikan's Bequest	69
The Smallest of Rooms	70

Shore Lines

Fog at Round Pond, Maine

See how the boats are compass to the wind,
Bows pointed east toward Muscongus Bay,
Taut on their moorings, slipped against the play
Of tides, their line as of a single mind.
They set their sterns to evergreen and rock
That steeps and slides the shore into the sea,
They dream of knowing hands, a liberty,
A rowing out of skiffs, untying knots.
But as the fog, warmed water's silver smoke
Rolls over them, investing row on row,
Their masts and hulls no longer purposed for,
The harbor and the harbored all are cloaked
In gray soft shapes like woodpiles under snow,
While dreams of sailing out remain ashore.

Watercolor Words

An india ink cursive trail of words
Accidently moistened, the writing blurred
Together, edges slurred into the shapes
Of clouds, or storm born foam crest waves to break
Across a fog-bound beach, its coastline lost
In mist whose alchemy will render soft
All definition, or perhaps become
An antique map whose foreign names for home
Are now illegible, its fabric just
One careless unfolding from precious dust
In tremble hands, or poetry at best
Washed into a sepia palimpsest.

Waiting for the Red-winged Blackbirds

The beach is here a fingernail of sand
Washed by slight murmur tides of slate blue sea,
Barely a walking width, the shore's line bends
Toward an assembly of common reeds,
Wisp feather-headed russet stalks of staves
For a flock of bishops or blackbirds' brake
To perch when they appear. Today, the waves
You hear, the wind you feel are all that take
Up this monotony of March, the sky
Longing for returning birds flashing their
Red shoulders in the cane, staccato cries
Of greeting and of warning 'cross the air
When dark arrival, ritual mating
Signify an end to winter waiting.

A Little Boat, My Heart

A little boat, my heart,
Curved gothic to its bow
From starboard and from port,
To plow an ocean's row,

To turn the slightest waves
Brief furrows, to expose
The undersea, a spray
Of foam, a path to lose

Across the sea astern,
A dip and sweep of oars,
Cut circles that become
Skin smooth and disappear.

My heart, a little boat
Set on your waves of skin
That on my voyage out
I cross to cross again

A sea of passages
To India, a rise
And fall of tides. It is
Moon driven. From your eyes

Glances like quick fishes
Leaping, circles that part
Still water round, kisses,
A little boat, my heart.

Nohaval Cove, County Cork

Long down an overgrown and unmarked lane
Trees branch a tattered cover, bristle-maned
Hedgerows scratch and scrape before it opens
Between wildflower slopes as it descends
To the sea, one rise a grass-swept scramble
Up to sudden cliffs, the other bramble
Ledges, footholds, shelves of loose, rubble stone
From ancient watcher towers, unmade bones
Of ruined cautions above a narrow
Cove slid under brae and bluff, a shallow
Treacherous peat black water's waves to wear
Round sharp-shinned shards of blunt Irish coast sheared
Off into a secret landfall for boats
Of rebels, smugglers, lovers, come about
Conspiracy, so willing to risk all
To be ashore, or gone, among these shoals.
On this rock-angled edge of afternoon
Rain drifter clouds tear open where alone
Together, we keep watch to hear the breach
Of water through the cove, catch bright patches
Of clover, mayweed, trefoil up the hill,
Feel fresh wind rising in the gathered still,
Inhale the earth's, the sea's perfume, the air's
Uncivil, unpretending atmosphere
Breathing benediction over traces
Of past danger, deception, or disgrace,
Unclaimed memories, shadows of lovers,
Watchmen, treasoners and thieves, hover
Here where impassioned lives, set sudden down,
Are held in this embrace and then sent on.

On Pemaquid Beach: The Lost Soldier

He lay not fifty sea-breeze meters from the shore,
Half-buried under sand in his smart uniform,
His company moved on, the terror wild of war
Silenced, wounds uncertain, identity unknown.

Imagine Anzio, or Normandy, a place
Of debarkation, small landing crafts' bobble run
Into the shallows, a sudden jolt of ramps, waist
Deep water where morning's discovered blood ran warm.

He grasps a Browning Automatic in both hands
As if to fire toward an unseen enemy
Who could not hold the beach and falling back inland
Would reassemble in a camouflage of trees.

Then as the dunes were cleared, the armies' heated joust
Come to an end, brave talk of battles went among
His comrades when he unnoticeably fell, lost
In the gathering of toys children carried home.

Cloth of Gold: Round Pond, Maine

The Pond stands mantled in a cloth of gold,
A shoulder-shifting light breeze borne brocade's
Bright threads of gossamer in wavy folds
Surround the smooth hulled boats that tip and sway
Their finger masts, gauges, starboard to port,
Of wind direction and velocity
For mariners ashore before they start
To row toward moorings on a golden sea.

Once, in a world five hundred years ago,
Two princes, France and England, stood opposed,
Rivals in splendored sets of royal show
Known after as 'The Field of Cloth of Gold,'
But here where wind and water ever be
As changeable in mood as princes are,
No one may long recall this drapery
That is the sea's quick reflect of a star.

From Berkeley to Boston
On the California Zephyr
and the Lake Shore Limited

Hear, in the middle distance at the edge of town,
Train whistles signaling the long rails headed east,
Skirting the Bays, crossing wetlands, up mountain bone,
Straight over desert flats, threading a shoulder's crease
Of gorgeous canyons, rail tied to rail, welded track
Stitching the herded prairies' Mississippi tear,
In a fan of yards switched out to great lakes that back
Small farms, by rivers' fall down to a final shore.
The rails like nerves are endless pathways, constructs
   through
Landscapes of water, stone and earth, continental,
Uninterrupted circuits whose locomotion
Carries us toward pleasure's beaches, past sorrow's snow,
Like routes within ourselves where touch may travel
Its unbroken line of way to the heart's ocean.

Good morning, Alice!

An early look out from the starboard deck
Across a seascape dark as any deep
Beneath a sky still keeping, seeming night,
Northward a horizontal glimmering
Along an unseen coast, a thousand fallen
Stars, a motionless parade of paper lanterns
Strung where the shore road edges to the bridge
Outlined in faerie lights, a magic door
To some enchanted world resolving into
Pylons and cable as a small escort,
Orange-tipped meringue clouds, floats overhead
Through a sky blushing dusky rose cooling
To powder blue somewhere beyond Coney Island.
Red channel buoys toll their morning bells
As the ship, slicing water like a plow
In the soft spring earth, slides, barely, under
The Verrazano into harbor, past
Your apartment in Brooklyn. Good morning,
Alice! Dead ahead, on Manhattan, rise
Indifferent towers mounting the morning
Watch on the Battery. To either side
Over the rivers of separation
Wires stretch on the looms of the city,
Weaving disparity into New York.
From an eastern ocean underworld
The sun, freshly washed and slightly salty,
Getting a light from the green lady's torch,
Transforms opposing walls: aluminum,
Steel, stone, glass into superficial dreams,
A lost city of gold, ship's shiny brass,
We furrow up the Hudson on the tide,
Nudged and nosed by cocky pit-bull tugs
Into a midtown berth at Fifty-second
Street, slim leaders tossed ashore, hawsers pulled
From the muddy river, slipped heavily
Over their iron stanchions, lines winched taut,
We are tied again to America.

Goat Island, County Waterford

A path's way worn through cliffs and castles down,
Down from pinked clover meadows to a plain
Of tides and tide-pools where a Celtic moon
Draws up the warm-edged sea, drawn down again

To create an amphitheatre, stranded
Pools, isolated rocks, the failing waves
Near silent breakers' whisper to the sand,
A beach for sweethearts' walks, of children's caves.

Then further out a solitary spur
Of climbing stone, grass crowned, a place to stand
To gather in the sweep and slope of shore
Exposed as ocean's sometime underland,

To ask for nothing more but tide to drown
Our way's return, abandon us awhile
Beyond the reach of company or town,
Whose obligations clamor and beguile.

We shall be well cut off, left to our own,
Unable and unwilling to attend
The civil world, as 'til the tide comes down,
We may pretend to this world without end.

A Dream of Fishes

An iron sea breaks bright beside the boats
From random light poured through a sieve of cloud,
A shimmer brilliance of fine jewels cut
By wind in wave as if someone had ploughed
Dark fields and turned up diamonds or a horde
Of hidden coins, a miser treasury
From some forgotten king whose wealth was stored
Too deep for public generosity.
The fisher folk on this astounding sea
Might wish to haul aboard this silver gleam
Whose provenance is miracle and faith,
But if the wind lie still, or suddenly
Clouds fill the sky, the heart wear doubt, then dreams
Of riches are for fishes underneath.

Beach Stones

Like jewels in an ancient kingdom's crown
Half-buried under sand small smooth stones lie
Sea-washed brilliant to catch a wander eye
At the retreat of tides lovers come down
To walk along the silvered water's edge
Its broken repetitions whispering
"Again," "again," imagining a ring
Made from one gleaming fragment on the beach.
But its remove will dry and dull the stone
Deprived of its refreshment from the sea
And now no further reverie may serve,
As we, displaced, dull with affection gone
That brought us to a certain brilliancy
In being swept each day through tides of love.

Benevolence

See how the fractured stones are worn to smooth
Within the ground or tumbled by the sea,
Sharp fragments broken off, a sudden heave
Of rock shaken loose, displaced and blindly
Carried in moving fields of ice whose spread
Turned to retreat millennia ago,
Moraine debris becoming dust buried
In a decay of wander plants to grow
New forest, while others left on the shore
In jumbled heaps will wear each other down
To grains of sand from ocean's tides and storm,
All angularity slow coming round.
How kind the sea, benevolent the earth,
Was it for love these stones were so unroughed?

September Evening at Randlett Pond

The wind is etching currents on the pond
Out of the south, or contrary, come round
From north, a metallic surface pounded
To repoussé, a stir of air close in
Scattering those images of trees lined
Up along the shore, the softest designs
Of clouds undone among the waves, the sun,
Which gilded just the forest's tips at dawn,
Here for abbreviated time, then down
Behind a ridge under a gibbous moon,
A whirl of stars, a solitary loon
Marks with his startle cry the summer gone
As bats fly noiselessly defying dusk
Becoming dark, seemingly at their best
While other creatures sense a shape of loss
When night will mask the where of untamed sounds
And days go gray on gray on without end,
The wind still etching currents on the pond.

A Walk at World's End

At World's End there may be only silence
Left by the wind, or a quiet of birds,
The ruffled feathers of the waves long since
Ashore, slipping like hastily breathed words
From confessions through rock dark crevices,

The ocean calmed in salt marshes, cat-tails
Rise to a lingering pink moon, russet
Meadow grass is winter matted down, snails
Not awake, white oaks' discarded leaves spread
Underfoot, mud imprints from March's trail

Walkers cover an Avalonian
Geology. How deep, how deep, the play
Of basalt and ash Merlin's magicians
Made with fire and ice to mold the Bay
Of the Massachuset glacial drumlins

In overcoats of trees, unimagined
Fields, settlement, a city on a hill,
Or Olmstead's dream of springing green again
As we spend an infinitesimal
Forever in the silence at world's end.

First and Last Paintings, Juxtaposed

"The Coast of Cornwall"

Dark waves come curling from a spiral core
As they run in to cliffs, tips white with froth,
A sudden spittle spewed from angry mouths,
One after one approaching Cornwall shore.

Fierce breakers then, and still fierce, sea and stone
Confronting one another, wearing smooth,
Rash, roughest elements in making love
Come crashing on before the pebbles moan.

See how a palette knife laid on the sea,
Breaking on, off, this verticality
Of coast, as we, drawn unavoidably
Together, could agree to disagree.

"Sea Shells"

Seas' shells, a beachcomber's sand-locked prizes
In a studio, lovely, driest bone
Curled chamber's amber alabaster tones
Beneath a carapace it despises

But cannot do without, as ancient walls,
Rounded towers about Byzantium
Whose murex purple dyes the ghosts that come
To seek a livelihood in marbled halls

Empty as gathered shells in layered paint,
Set here together in a measured calm
Far from the restless sea, relentless storms,
As we, in later lives, withdrew complaint.

After words

Corner to corner, forty years apart
Between the raucous sea, the gathered shells,
Lives measured out in passion's ebbs and swells,
As silence after swiftly beating hearts.

Reluctance

See where a white geometry of sail
Mainsail and jib bow taut with sea's salt air,
Waves cut from bow to stern their wider trail
That disappears with distance to repair
While at the tiller an intentioned arm
Sets certain course between two slips of shore
To change great liberty for harbor calm
Only to come about, sail out once more
As if reluctant at descent of day
And summer's time finally to return
To sheltered moorings, winter's company
With other boats, imagining to stay
At sea, to come about into the wind
Sailing away under forever's lee.

Iamque Vale
(And now, Farewell)

Iamque vale
Virgil, Georgics IV.497

There is no turning back behind the calendar,
The world before the world of Orpheus denied
Eurydice, music fading, fallen too far
For recollection or return to the bed's side
Where you lie in death's pajamas while round you dance
A sarabande's hushed parade of farewell sayers,
Knowing the diagnosis, confirmed, of cancer,
The consolation of morphine, perhaps prayers.
When Orpheus sang, Pluto and Persephone
Wept, Hell ceased to be hell, six-eyed Cerberus slept,
The wheel of Ixion went still, Eurydice
Just four or five steps from the garden which she kept
With her companions when the Fates portioned her way
Again under the world, forgetting living dreams
Of weddings and weekends, murmuring, "Iamque
Vale," and now farewell, whatever we have been
We took too lightly, this descent of darkness breaks
Irrevocable exile from experience
To memory whose shadow characters may take
A final bow as ghosts, the rest is abstinence.

Shelves of War:
The Reading Room of the Cork City Library

There is no war that is not made a book,
Fierce combat in the air, at sea, on plain or slope
Played in vast theatres of manoeuvres,
Rage angry worlds pressed between hard covers,
Though pages' printed letters not enough
To count fatalities, nor photographs
Reveal where deep unfathomable hurt
Makes secret mutilation of the heart,
Those jaunty cigarette-to-lips regards
Of sometime courageous, sometime coward
Conscripts a uniform camouflage, doubts'
Disguises, before orders to move out.

Here, in Cork City's Library Reading
Room no one is gravely wounded, bleeding,
No shouting, moaning, crying, cursing heard,
Where words of war now are the wars of words,
Standing shoulder to shoulder, an array
Of titled spines: *Bloody April, D-Day,
Monte Cassino, Stalingrad, Berlin,
Paschendale, Gallipoli, The Fallen,*
Fallen quiet, in perfect order still
As on parade before some general,
A shelved review, a brief roll call of ghosts,
Bound in silence to gather civic dust.

Fire and Ash

Hickory and oak, fire's wood, dry split and stacked
Beside the porch keeps second summer in the sun,
Memory of shadows' shade in an ancient tract
Of forest filtering a dapple daylight down
Onto a feather bed of fern has slipped away
Through seasons come temporarily like children
Visiting, promising return whether we stay
Here or not, where once strong hands cradled, carried in
Wood for the house, setting it on irons to draw
Up flame, suffuse a room with its incense and warm
For tea and talk, a gentle poultice for the raw
Hibernal days of dreaming under eiderdown.
This wood untouched, its splintered edges smooth to rain
Split quarters' fresh cut odors lost, a glowing red
Of dying embers held unseen within the pain
That would become an urn of ashes in their stead.

Window Boxes, 34 rue des Plantes 1996/2009

Long ago perhaps, we were tenants here,
Time to unremember the furniture's
Apartment, *premier étage*, second floor,
Grey facade, marbled door of thirty-four
Rue des Plantes where the *"Cent-huit"* bistro bar,
Boulangerie, le Moulin Vert, keep their
Familiar faces to the street as I
Walk close from my hotel, a careful eye
Counts three shutter windows whose ledges held
Clay window planters we had purchased, filled
With October foliage, winter fir,
Jewel primroses, summer's brilliant stir
Of knock-your-socks-off red geraniums,
In a year's sojourn the briefest garden.

Now in two thousand nine one box remains,
Empty, untended in October rain,
But less its emptiness calls out to me
Than its unwonted singularity,
For you who bought and planted flowers there
Have come, like calendars, to disappear
And what made blossom once against dark stone
Has faded to a reverie of one.

The Last Time You Saw Paris (2001)

The last time you saw Paris was July,
A Tuesday morning market, rue Breteuil,
Set out its produce as if God's pardon
Restored us to our primeval garden
Of creation when shadow dapple shade
In the Luxembourg was paradise made
Of summer afternoons' green lawn of chairs,
Empty with invitations in a stir
Of bees, to stay, to sit, to rest, to read,
To leave on a parade of chestnut trees
To walk in Montparnasse among the graves'
Visitors where only the dead may live.
 A Sunday's music, bright organ notes come
Dancing down from the soaring vaults of stone
At St. Eustache, in the dark Madeleine
An English choir, eucharist again
In St. Pierre Montrouge. Out in the parks
A little picnic, *quiche* and apple tart
Eaten by the Seine at the Vert Galant,
The Trocadéro. Curious time spent
In the *passages'* shops for souvenirs,
Yours for a doll's house, mine a chevalier,
In the Petit Palais ordinary
Objects from excavations at Pompeii
Revealing closest life so far away
By centuries, their temporary stay
Like our own, enough to gather light
And dust, to learn from brief remains how slight
The moment is before the die are cast
To hold what may forever soon be lost.

Familiar Gestures

A mixing bowl of clay, blue womb of earth
Cradles the flour whose white dust covers
The counter, a snowy ring underneath
The bowl. Your left arm curves like a lover's

Around the outer rim. Its inward curve
Nestled against your aproned body's own
Soft rise. You stand there by the warming stove,
Your right hand holding a rough wooden spoon

To stir, beating assembled ingredients
To a winter afternoon's alchemy
Of batter whose right measured elements
Combine out of their singularity

Under your hands, small wrists and arms grown strong
In these familiar gestures that linger
On the pages of your recipes turned brown,
Scraping the sticky spoon with your finger,

Your finger with the spoon repeatedly
Until the batter comes to breaking off
Into a patient bowl, reluctantly,
As in that letting go when lovers touch.

Now in my kitchen life, these memories
Cling to the weathered wooden spoon I hold,
Their weight no greater than infinity
To drop and fold themselves within the bowl.

Before You Left

Before you left, all the kitchen cupboards
Were filled with honey sweet and savory
Provisions of your absent love, stored,
Too, in pine bureau drawers, carefully
Laid out on soft linens' pillow cases,
Draped over closet hangers' patient frames,
Set forever in familiar faces
Smiled from a gathered crowd of pictured names,
Found in the arms of comfortable chairs,
Glazed on the circles of our dinner plates,
Hidden as random sighs on wooden stairs,
Wound up within the clock's tick-tocking gait
Making a measure of your lost presence
Whose souvenirs linger in affection
To surround my living as an incense
That burns and smolders its way to Heaven.

Birches in a Country Churchyard

Suppliant birches, planted in your name,
Bend over frozen ground,
White bark arches carry a fall of caked
Whiter snow that surrounds
The darkest branches. Tall, sturdier beech,
Oak, chestnut, maple, rise
Coated with snow's flake frosting as they reach
Into an ice gray sky
While conifers nearby become snow cones
By letting drop their arms
Drawing evergreen blankets close, a home
To sparrows in the storm.

Of all the trees, the birches are most bowed
And burdened by the weight
Of snow, a parabolic overload
Of crystal, single flakes
Weightless as thoughts, accumulated here
In heaviness to bear
As crowded thoughts may weigh us down with cares
That will not disappear,
Unless, within, there is intent to spring
Back like birches, to shake
The snow, the cares away, a purposing
In bending not to break.

After Isaiah 10:19
"And the remaining trees of his forests will be so few that a child could write them down."

If there were so few trees
A child could write them down,
No bears would climb for bees,
No wolf lie with the lamb.

If there were so few trees,
The rain that fell to ground
Would run away to seize
The land that grows the corn.

If there were so few trees
No shadow shade of brown
Would cool below the leaves
That sang the four winds' song.

If there were so few trees
Desert would come to sown,
And bony mountain's knees
Wear smooth under the sun.

If there were so few trees
The wrinkled earth must frown,
For there would never be
A child to write them down.

The Roman Amphitheatre at Arles

At Arles, the Roman amphitheatre counts
Two rows of sixty arches in ellipse
Embracing sand, where beasts and men act out
A spectacle of death, now morning kissed
By sunlight, its freshly restored facade
Of fossil limestone glows a tawny warm
Of re-creation as if masons made
Again this antique city by the Rhone.
But look, within an arch a patch of green
Grows in between cleaned stone, wind-ferried seed
Taking surprising root where moisture, air,
Light and a little dust revive the dream
Of Nature to invade, conquer with weed
Whatever marks of passage we build here.

Night Watch, Amsterdam

A stroopwafel moon
Wafer in the mouth
Of the night, a white
Ruff collar of lace
On a black gowned sky,
A searchlight dancing
In the Prinsengracht,
An "O"pening to
Evade the SS
At two a.m. as
The moon pauses on
Westerkerk steeple,
An inverted point
Of exclamation,
Of rendezvous for
The ghosts of Rembrandt
Van Rijn and Anne Frank.
What will the warty
Moon-faced old man say
To Abraham's child?
Have we both survived
In our self-portraits?
Curiosity
Grows queues of tourists
Climbing the steep stairs
Within our buildings,
Will they wonder at
This moon, as round as
June, bells from the *kerk*
That chime the silence
With their rhymes as we
Assume our night watch?

1960 Wedding Photograph

The sun is west, it is late afternoon
Where figures cast long shadows on the lawn,
They seem a very best in black and white
Against the dark of trees, the August light
Within a setting kept forever still
A wedding party's photograph reveals
Young men not old enough for formal wear,
The women in their taffeta, mature,
A bride in white, her prince, maids, groomsmen tall
Over a petite flower girl, all smile
As if those gathered here on summer's green
Were flowered guards before a house of dreams.

A first and last reunion wedding day
With separate tomorrows when decades
Will pass into a reckoning, the bride,
Two of her bridesmaids and a groomsman die,
Two maids and two men are divorced, the groom,
His best man widowed as survivors come
Through half a century where they remain
Ungathered but still in the picture's frame
To celebrate this anniversary
Of light and shadows in a scenery
Where they were careless, carefully exposed
Before the camera's shutter eye was closed.

Anniversary - 1961

I gave my heart a pretty pair of doves
A twelve-month passage from our wedding day,
Gold-eyed, sienna figures smooth as love,
One saw the ground, the other looked away.

A twelve-month passage from our wedding day
We sailed aboard a Queen to England bound,
A gift of doves for anniversary,
One looked to sea, the other back to land.

Gold-eyed, sienna figures smooth as love
For two score years and more they were displayed
On mantles in the houses where we lived,
One saw the hearth, the other looked away.

I keep, dear heart, the pair of mourning doves
Through way-worn years of memory as mine
Here on this anniversary of love,
One for the ground, and one who looks behind.

Love's Fire

Love's Fire

First, gather a quick kindling of kisses
To set about the stacked wood of desire,
Then striking a chemic match of wishes
Bring life to imaginary fire

Where flame and smoke rise in a chimney's 'scape,
Light and veil of mutual attraction
Drawn up as one together who will take
Seduction's straw to enkindle passion

To burst into an overwhelming warm,
A blaze of such delight, intensity
That skin is ample cover in the room
Its blushes seeming incendiary.

Then as the fire dies, the darker hearth
Of glowing embers spends a sun soft heat
Within that quiet afterwards beneath
An ash-gray blanket banked for dreams and sleep.

Tomorrow when the fire's place gives off
Its dark, uncivil, bittersweet perfume,
Shadow odors may inspiration serve
To build another fire in the room.

Birthday Greetings VI: The Riverway

out of a muddy river, a water's way
of creation, a dream of ponds and paths,
an ocean waiting at the end of a stream
at the beginning, a meander chain
of light-catcher pools strung together
like rough-cut jewels on a ripple necklace
where broad salt marshes once spread
over a brackish flood, now routed
between sculpted banks, cleared of underbrush
and shadowed in stands of beech and oak.

it was when October slept in the trees
and the river's reeds remembered summer
sunlight filtering down to the water
where ducks and geese, swans and herons
swam and flew into the evening
on a night halfway to winter
you and i sat on a bench in this house of leaves,
inlaid with river, a ceiling of stars,
i asked you to imagine forever,
and when i asked again, you said yes.

so you brought me your dream of creation,
channeling my meanderings
clearing banks of overgrown intentions
designing paths through a landscape
planting brave trees into the future
settling shallows with tawny reeds
stirring the air with the wings of water birds
making an emerald necklace of our lives,
an intentionally civilized wilderness
forty years before we came to the ocean.

"Love One Another"
-Inscription on the Richardson/Barber head-stone in Riverview Cemetery, Brunswick, Maine

Verdigris lichen patches wear on rose-pink stone
Inscribed with ancestral names, their mottled cover
Whispering to its host, "Why should we be alone
Where it is written in the rock, 'Love one another'?"

At Riverview, July's sweet grass goes August brown,
Breeze off the Androscoggin bends it close over
Open ground, settled, ancestral bone, where the sown
Whispers to dry earth, "Do we love one another?"

So is the stone itself heavy in Brunswick soil,
The weight of granite pressing, whispering, "Lovers
Are we in gravity's embrace; how could we fail
To follow its demand to love one another?"

What of Henry and Cecilia? Were they once bound
Like lichen to a host of stone, grass in hover
Over thirsty earth, headstones to compliant ground,
As they whispered a bond to love one another?

Will someday visitors who walk among these stones
Down dusty tracks between the grave rows discover
Cut in as neat, as cold, as sure as death is done,
The whisperers' command to love one another?

Hearts of Stone
*From an Etruscan Sarcophagus in the
Boston Museum of Fine Arts*

Eyes have the gauge of eyes,
The possibilities
Of lovers face to face,
Side to in an embrace
Of arms extended touch,
An alabaster couch,
Pillows underneath their
Profile heads, careful hair,
An earring in her ear,
His beard are all they wear,
Her fingers curled about
His neck, he reaches out
To her shoulder, his arm,
Resting over her own,
Half hides her breast's brief rise.
Between thin sheets their thighs
Curve out to taper in
A heart, a valentine,
As their anatomies
Are lost in drapery.

They are about to speak,
To kiss, but cannot break
The distance that's imposed
On their affection, close
Lovers, whose hearts of stone
Are almost, never one,
Unlike ourselves; you wear
Only blue earrings here
My beard is my attire,
Where our bodies' fire,
Consuming and consumed,
Is transience presumed
When muscle hearts beat one
A moment, and are gone.

A Geology of Love

What compass will we use to measure out
The strike and dip of bedding, trend of faults,
The rake of slickenlines, the strata set
Beneath our surfaces, earth, skin; impulse
Invades the strike and dip of bedding down
To obviate or emphasize the trend
Of faults, slips scarcely measured in our own
Tectonic plates shifting toward an end,
Or ending in a shift of tell-tale signs,
A rake of slickenlines conformably
Overlain with love, a fusion refined
By water, wind, fire, a geology
Whose entire sequence of progression
Represents continuous transgression.

Shall We Not Kiss?

Shall we not kiss
Not break this silence from our lips?

Shall we not glance
Not blind a partner in the dance?

Shall we not speak
Not spend sharp arrows of heart's ache?

Shall we not hear
Not hoard the blushing sounds of care?

Shall we not scent
Not arm soft odors with intent?

Shall we not taste
Not salt the meat awaiting feast?

Shall we not touch
Not breech frontiers barbed with "enough?"

Shall we not sleep
Not drown in dreams' steep dreaming deep?

Shall we not love
Not seize desire's gilded trove?

Shall we not mate
Not rob the world of celibate?

Shall WE not be
Not die into eternally?

Against such mystery as this,
Shall we not kiss?

Is There A Rose?

Is there a Rose by any other name?
Rosa, rosae, rosae, rosam, rosa,
Her first declension singular remains

To please the ear, the tongue that will declaim
Her essence for the hand, the eye, the nose,
Is there a Rose by any other name?

Predicate Rose the subject of love's flame,
Possessive Rose of thorns that pierce to flow,
Rosa, rosae, rosae, rosam, rosa,

Indirect Rose for whom I shall obtain
An object rose though I might her love lose,
Is there a Rose by any other name?

Rose prepositional who may explain
By, with or from capricious acts, God knows,
Rosa, rosae, rosae, rosam, rosa,

Will Rose declining me come back again
Or will her love lie in the grave's dark close?
Is there a Rose by any other name,
Rosa, rosae, rosae, rosam, rosa.

Birthday Greetings V: At the Berlin Zoo

Did you imagine me as I imagined you?
Did I imagine you as you imagined me?
September, early afternoon, the Berlin Zoo,
The whole creation which we saw so differently.

You understood the animals themselves, wild, free,
Did you imagine me as I imagined you?
Among the curious primates we disagreed,
September, early afternoon, the Berlin Zoo.

I saw them, creatures in captivity and caged,
You understood the animals themselves, wild, free,
It was a timid, tired, tourists' war we waged,
Among the curious primates we disagreed.

You saw in nature wonderful simplicity,
I saw them, creatures in captivity and caged,
Lincoln Park, Chicago, a childhood memory,
It was a timid, tired, tourists' war we waged

Under late summer sun, the lindens' scented shade,
You saw in nature wonderful simplicity,
Perhaps all I wanted was some ice cream, I said,
Lincoln Park, Chicago, a childhood memory.

We keep ourselves together down the afternoon
Under late summer sun, the lindens' scented shade,
At last at ease again with evening's dinner come
Perhaps all I wanted was some ice cream, I said.

Each to the other still imperfectly aligned,
We keep ourselves together down the afternoon,
Whatever notions ran untamed are now confined,
At last at ease with evening's dinner come.

Did I imagine you as you imagined me?
Each to the other still imperfectly aligned,
The whole creation which we saw so differently,
Whatever notions ran untamed are now confined.

Did you imagine me as I imagined you?
Did I imagine you as you imagined me?
September, early afternoon, the Berlin Zoo,
The whole creation which we saw so differently.

Col des Vents 2001

Warm morning slides over a kitchen's window sill
Filling last evening's empty dusk green bottle, still
On the table, a soft chartreuse shoulder darkly stained
With fermentation's stubborn traces which remain
Congealed against the slope of glass, a Rorschach test
Of sediment, evidence of a summer passed
Within the Col des Vents whose white-capped Pyrenees
Break in an azure sky and spears of cedar trees
Rise to defend a village where rows of gnarled vines
Descend a mountain pass the wind has named the wine.
The year is two thousand one, as travelers down
From Paris to the familiar dust red brown
Earth of the Midi have come to beg or borrow
Sun from ancient scattered stones and vineyards, all now
Remembered in a glass held sideways, where I see
In the Corbières the luminous transparency
Of your transparency, a blushing carmine red
Of faces flushed when love has taken them to bed,
A biting rush of taste whose lingering bouquet
Is rough as pinpricks on the palate, a dancing play
Of tannin over tongues, one body held within
Another, a summons of musty grapes autumn
Ripe, brought from my cellar, breathing the current air
And held within a glass to taste of you still here.

The Chapel of Saint Gabriel near Tarascon

Hid in a dusty-green of olive trees,
A small gray weathered limestone chapel-church,
Its ancient walls worn through nine centuries
Of winter rain, dry Mistral wind, an arch
Brief shelter for the angel Gabriel
Hovering over Eve in déshabille
Beside self-conscious Adam where they fell
Beneath the serpent-circled apple tree.
Here off the road, unseen by passers-by,
With sun alone to light the darkened bays,
Age wears these traces of rude masonry,
The builders and believers gone their ways
Into silence before the olive grove
Grew silvered leaves to hide God's naked love.

The Courtyard at the Faculty of Medicine, Montpellier, France

There is a sense of passage in the wall,
Traces of gothic arcs held in the stones
Of Benedictine monks, masons recalled
In a row of arches whose narrow bones
Of faith kept only atmosphere for skin
Where holy passengers in sandals stirred
The dust about the cloister's close, closed in
God's own embrace yet closed out to the world.

Perhaps within this ghostly tracery
The lives of those once faithful cloistered here
Are held as close as recent memory,
Their exits, entrances, still in the air
Where neither death nor stone may cause remove
And morticed traces of a distant time's
Architecture of deliberate love
Disclose what is beyond the world's design.

The Pont du Gard

The day lies brilliant under broken clouds,
As we approach midday the Pont du Gard,
We have been traveling on Roman roads

To join some million other passers-by
Walking along the Gardon's mirror sky
Passing into shadows of masonry.

Later we'll eat beside the poplar trees,
Our terrace table's view enough to see
The limestone arches' hollow symmetry,

Lesser from greater, bridge to aquifer,
Ascending arcs whose weighted shoulders bore
Water from Uzès over the valley floor

Two thousand years ago straight on to Nîmes
Where lunch was olives, bread and wine,
Like ours - in France, what changes stays the same.

The stones, ourselves, held by no mortar here
But love, the water's conduit only air,
Its broken ends, like lives, invite repair

Or not, better to leave things as they are,
Dressed antique stone, the heated atmosphere
Keep what is old for what is new, both dear.

I Did Not Meet Her in the Morning

I did not meet her in the morning,
I did not meet her at midday,
The afternoon was edging evening
As she came up the river's way.

She did not name me in the morning,
She did not name me at midday,
But passing afternoon to evening,
She called my name as questions say.

We spoke of lives apart in morning,
Of lovers taken at midday,
We spoke of afternoon and evening,
Of how October stood from May

Of roses blooming autumn mornings,
Of winter's blinding bright midday,
Of afternoons' long shadowed evenings
Before the light is swept away.

Now she has come for me as morning,
Hers is the brilliance of midday,
As afternoon slips into evening
She keeps the dark, the night, at bay.

Thanksgiving

Thanksgiving

Air cuts like kitchen knives through November,
We do not meet our neighbors out-of-doors,
By five PM, clouds burn down to embers,
Old Adirondack chairs sit out ignored.

One shortened day rubs against another,
Cold branches scratch gnarled fingers on the sky,
Small children raise mitten hands to others,
We light pale candles for festivity,

Great preparations for small assembly,
Beside extended tables open chairs,
Elbows to elbows touch, eye catches eye,
Grace is a murmur silence in the stir.

A vintage wine uncorked for brotherhood
Offerings of planting, growth and harvest,
Familiar odors, customary food,
A thieving clock forgotten for the feast

With conversation turning round the year,
Warm serving dishes pass from hand to hand,
Acknowledgment of those who once were here,
Thanks given for this company returned.

St Patrick's Hill

As I walked up St Patrick's Hill
I saw the valley's crowded town
Of bridges, steeples, shops and mall,
A grit of buildings, dust blown down
The narrow streets with muffle sound
Of motor cars and pepper rain,
Gray River Lee's tidewater bound
For Cobh, the sea and back again.
There are a hundred steps to climb
In fours and fives beside the road,
A strong heart's pounding steep incline
To reach the top, the view abroad
Of wearing hills, new houses keen
To scramble up like weeds that grow
Toward ridges spread a gold and green
Of fields edged out in trees whose rows
Define the countryside. Here all
Is tarmac, walls, curbstone and walk,
Paint yellow parking lines that fall
Into the business ways of Cork.
And after coming up I thought
Of Saint Augustine's paradigm
Of two great cities, one of God,
The other filled with humankind,
Between the city and the hill,
Closer to Heaven, breathlessly
I choose the heights and climb on still
To Lansdowne Court for scones and tea.

Waiting for Snow

An odor of smoke rising in the house
Through open windows, out-of-doors, next door,
Sharp sirens bite the night, the day as close
As bursts of punctured, shattered glass before

A masque of firemen break the breezeway
Open to descend, carrying hoses,
To the cellar's sudden underworld. They
Emerge, the fire out, leaving losses

To an inventory of adjusters.
Smart red white and blue engines and cruisers
Melt into a few, curious clusters
Of neighbors, passers-by invent a news.

Blindfolded by a board of carpenters,
The house exhales an incense of carbon,
Abandoned by owners become renters,
A wildness will entertain their garden

All summer as the rain becomes July
Among discarded screens and tumbled chairs,
Grass shot up uncustomarily high,
A ruined city from a distant war.

No husband, wife play work, their light banter
Moving the afternoons towards rest, to take
A glass of wine. Silence is the matter
When maples scatter leaves that none will rake

Or feel a householders' unspoken pride
In ordered lawn, the border flowers' show,
Disorder here awaits the slip and slide
Of an obliterating storm of snow.

Snowbound

The tree was stripped of every elegance,
A radiant star, black threads of white corn
And cranberries, pale candles, ornaments
Of glass, small animals all taken down

And boxed away. Its forest self recalled
Once more, the tree's enchantment is unbound
To be, in whisper trails of needles' fall,
Borne from the house, set on the curbside ground

Where, joined by a second tree, together
They lay buried under snow, limb to limb,
Lovers hid in an embrace of weather
Before the sun would melt their cover thin

In March as still green branches are exposed
Like swimmers' arms rising above the sea,
So that the magic, which we had supposed
Forgotten, returned deliberately

To celebrate the solstice narrow gate
Of winter, Christmas tidings with no end,
For spring now, once imagined, is delayed
As snow is burying the trees again.

Legacy

New Hampshire made

The little green truck
With a little red cab

Dowel headlights
And chipped white bumper

Little white wheels
So round go round

Sturdy enough
To seat a child

Worn on its sides
By corduroy thighs

One brother
After another

Moved out and on
But not alone

Their company
A family

And a little green truck
With a little red cab

That little ones ride
By the ocean's side

In California.

Perpetual Calendar

An evergreen moroccan leather frame
Trimmed in a line of gilt and corner-worn
Presents a permanent address for change,
A calendar of dates not to be torn
Off or thrown away, reckoning a past,
Publishing a future on paper cards
Of months and days, turned, shuffled, and recast
Twelve times a year. These yellowing frayed shards
Of time and time again dissolving here
In waning moons and gyre stars declare
Constant rearrangement of forty years
Edges stained brown with the insistent wear
Of what will be, paradoxically
Pristine and lost in perpetuity.

Candlemas (February 2nd)

We are come halfway from winter's solstice
Toward spring's equality of day with night,
Crossing to February where the splice
Of darkness is unwound from threads of light,
This quarter's fabric a widening spread
Of visibility when tumuli
Of snow hold moisture for the buried dead
Dry ground beneath my window's picture eye.

Worlds away where Odysseus once sailed,
Pink and white blossoms, slopes of almond trees
Bloom with the year's first flowers, fragrant, frail
Petals falling beside the Middle Sea.
Here, further North, fresh snow has fallen through
The night, new candles, gathered offerings
To winter's god, blossom with fire to
Signify a lightening into spring.

Departure's Space
For my daughter, Cambridge to Berkeley

Let your departure be a space created
From the place, the traveler, in between
Here and there, now and then, a celibate
Roam and stray of dust star particles dreamed

Together, yesterday, voices' motion,
Bodies' touch, odors of perfume, glances,
Our Pacific to Atlantic Oceans'
Continental separation distance

Enough to raise over the weathered face
Of earth a memory palace from times
Of meeting, conversation, embrace,
A breeze-borne architecture, love's design

Where we may turn to return to repose
At days' end when the gardens' flowers close
As the sun's gold coin drops in a rosy
Bank of hills, then furthest stars appear close

Clustered, as we were once, although apart
As we are, light years in crossing to where
We share a silvered glimmer from the dark
Before we reckon all as souvenir.

Walking in Paris
in memory of James Robinson 1959-2004

James, alone, I have been walking with you
In the City of Light
As the sun rises from behind the heights
Of Chaumont, slanting through
The Marais, the courtyard of the Musée
Picasso, a small pool,
Sailboats in the Tuileries, chestnut cool
Paths in the shade sand gray
Luxembourg, along the sidewalk cafés,
Newspapers, journalists,
Read one another, afternoon kisses
Notre Dame's facade, a blaze
Of candles appears in restaurants, house lights
Dim at the Comédie
Française, over the Seine, Pont des Arts, we
Come out into the night
Filled with its ghosts, Molière, Napoléon,
Eloise, Beaumarchais,
Oscar Wilde, Camus, Piaf, Escoffier,
To Métro Robinson.

Paris en balade
A la mémoire de James Robinson, 1959-2004

James, seul, je t'accompagne à travers
Cette ville de soleil
Qui se lève le petit matin au delà des
Buttes Chaumont, sa lumière
Tombe dans le Marais, dans la cour du Musée
Picasso, sur les voiliers
Dans un bassin des Tuileries, aux marronniers
De sentiers ombragés
Du Luxembourg, autour des grands petits cafés
Ou journalistes, journaux se lisent
Les uns les autres, l'après-midi fait grosse bise
A Notre Dame, sur les quais
Les restaurants s'allument leurs tables de chandelles
Les lampes s'éteignent
A la Comédie française. Passons la Seine
Au Pont des Arts, la belle
Nuit pleine de fantômes, Molière, Napoléon
Héloise, Beaumarchais,
Oscar Wilde, Camus, Piaf, Escoffier,
Au Métro Robinson.

Ordinary Things: Pompeii

Ordinary things:
Hairpins, fibulae,
Clasping the fabric
Of quotidian life,
Frail, bright finger-rings,
Bracelets, catch-your-eye
Gold ear loops, the quick
Gift, husband to wife.

Ordinary things:
Bronze kitchen pots to
Cook, pans, sieves to sift,
To drain, to catch life's
Daily offerings,
Bread, meat, wine, so through
To love, the sweet gift
To husband from wife.

Ordinary things:
Hammers nails plumb line,
Weights, saw blades, planes,
To cut, to join, trim
New boards, smoothing
Rough edges, align
A door to remain
Set for her by him.

Ordinary things:
Fragments of frescoes,
Flowers, small birds for
Her, nature within,
Without, dark earth clings
To iron rakes, hoes,
By the open door
She has left for him.

Lessons in Greek
The beginning is half of the whole. -- Hesiod

Two primers
On a bookshelf of antiquities,
First Lessons in Greek,
First Greek Book,
To the left a leather spine
Stamped with Lydian gold,
A rough brown cloth cover
Like beaten ground at Marathon,
Signed by my father,
Bowdoin, Alpha Delta Phi,
March, Nineteen Hundred Thirty-Four,
On the right a red cloth cover
The color staining the robes
Of latecomers to the Assembly,
A title of black letters,
Dark as the entrance to Hades,
Signed by his son,
May, Nineteen Hundred Fifty-Three.
In Attic Greek such facts
Would be written in the aorist,
A tense of single past actions,
Or perhaps they could be
Written in the imperfect
Of past repeated actions
In exotic alphabets,
Mellifluous words,
Idiosyncratic grammar,
Whose knowledge is good,
And true and beautiful
As together we
Came separately
To learn imperfectly.

My Father's Grammar

His Blackwing pencils wrote a careful hand,
Corrections and suggestions written in
The margins of my text, verbs, subjects, stand
In agreement, wordy confessions thin
To clarity, commas become a pause,
Sometimes removed to carry actions, thought
Straight on, the subtle crafting of a clause
To be subordinate, right word use not
Ignored, so often mindful of careless
Repetition, modifiers misplaced
With civil paths to cross a wilderness
In search of self-expression, and grace
Within my manuscript the markings of
The unmistaken grammar of his love.

Victory Garden

Was it in forty-three
Or forty-four, or both?
The world was wrapped in war.
I watched my father march
Down Foster Street. He had
A spade, a hoe, a rake
To make a garden in
A winter skated field
Drying under the spring's
Incendiary bursts
Of flowers over this
Five-o'clock shadow man
Who taught Shakespeare and caught
The scent and feel of earth
Running soft in his hands.
He lined a string between
Two sticks, defined shallow
Trenches where he prepared
His ground. He would tear the
Picture packets at their
Corner, spreading seeds in
Tidy rows covered like
Combat dead in wartime
Cemeteries. Carrots
And radishes, string beans
Lettuce, peppers and peas,
A neighborhood of food,
Of coming victory
Imagined, summer's feast
Renewed, and then released
As autumn memory.

Ibn Khallikan's Bequest

Ibn Khallikan (d.1282 CE) was a prolific Moslem writer whose parings from his reed pens were used to heat the water to wash his corpse.
— C. Robinson, Islamic Historiography, 169

>Dear gentle readers and good friends,
>I leave the parings of my pens,
>Cut from the fertile river's reeds
>Swept, gathered, stored as fire seeds
>To heat the water when I fail,
>To wash my corpse from hair to nails.
>There's quantity enough for me
>To be washed warmly, carefully,
>That I may enter Paradise
>Clean and perfumed, or even spiced,
>Where all the faithful host will be
>Impressed with my prolixity.
>
>If you would write as much, don't ask
>Another to perform the task
>Of finding wood to heat the water
>To bathe you for the ever after,
>With Ibn Khallikan as guide,
>Or Robert Frost, Provide, Provide.

The Smallest of Rooms

In our beginnings, the smallest of rooms
One within another, dark, quiet, warm
Attending, appearing when cries surprise
A room lit large against our own small size,
Before we are wrapped up and carried 'home',
Set in a little room - one's very own
For growing up impatient to explore
Beyond the nursery, the second floor,
Downstairs, the yard, the neighborhood, the stars,
Choosing several rooms to claim as ours:
Some brief apartment changed against a house,
Whose many rooms invite especial use
With their distinctive furnishings and fonts
Of domesticity beyond account,
Until it seems too much and we retreat
To cozier quarters, an intimate
Pleasant, although diminished carapace,
Inevitably a room, a warm place
For repose under covers, once in bed,
The lights put out, door closed, someone has read
The Last Rites, now a wooden box, an urn
Makes for us, at the end, the smallest room.

Philip E. Burnham Jr. received the Arizona Quarterly's Prize for best poem, and the New England Poetry Club's Gretchen Warren Award in 2010 and 2012. His work was featured on Garrison Keillor's National Public Radio program, A Writer's Almanac. He is the author of four books of poetry including *My Neighbor Adam* (Mellen Press 2003), *Sailing from Boston* (Ibbetson Street Press 2003), *Housekeeping* (Ibbetson Street Press 2005), and *A Careful Scattering* (Cervena Barva Press 2007). A resident of Cambridge, Massachusetts, he was born in Rochester, New York, and grew up in New England.

COLOPHON

Headline type is ITC Zaph Chancery
Body type is 13 pt. Trumph Mediaeval

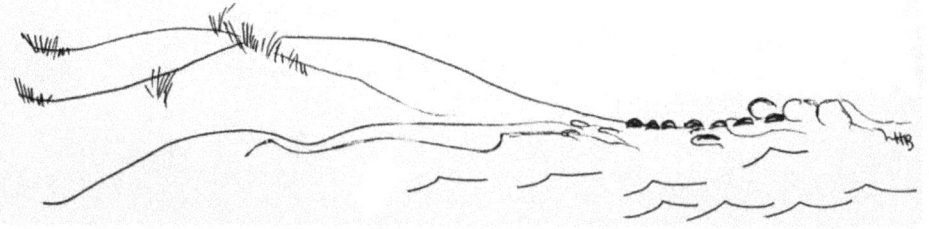

www.ingramcontent.com/pod-product-compliance
Lightning Source LLC
Chambersburg PA
CBHW031210090426
42736CB00009B/863